CHRISTMAS, CHRI:
Christmas

A Holiday Spectacular
Arranged for the Early Intermediate Pianist

JERRY RAY

To me, Christmas has always signified the beginning of something new … something fresh … something different. Perhaps it's the sense of urgency in anticipation of the New Year. Or maybe it's the crispness of the cold winter air and that unique energy we all seem to exhibit. It's with that spirit that I wrote this holiday spectacular.

Christmas, Christmas, Christmas is something new … something different. I've mixed together sacred and secular holiday favorites and added a few extra special surprises. For instance, there's a little of the *Messiah* hiding in one arrangement plus the hint of a well-known Johann Strauss melody in another. I've arranged "Away in a Manger" and "The First Noel" with a real distinctive contemporary flair. And "Jingle Bells," "Deck the Halls" and "We Wish You a Merry Christmas" add even more fun! All ten titles have something special worth discovering.

I hope this holiday spectacular is the beginning of something new… something fresh … something different for you. It has been for me. But before you run off to the keyboard, let me wish you and your entire family the warmest, happiest and most musical *Christmas, Christmas, Christmas* ever!

Enjoy!

Alfred

Music engraving: Nancy Butler
Cover photograph: © 1994 Cosmo Condina/Tony Stone Images

Silent Night

Music by Franz Grüber
Arranged by Jerry Ray

4

The First Noel

Traditional English Carol
Arranged by Jerry Ray

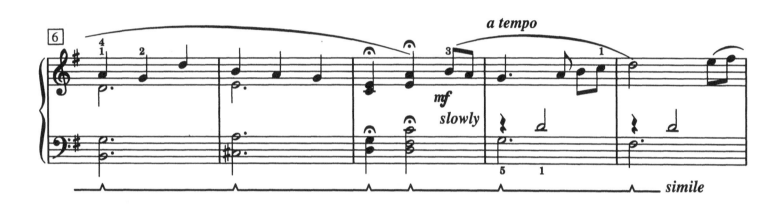

6

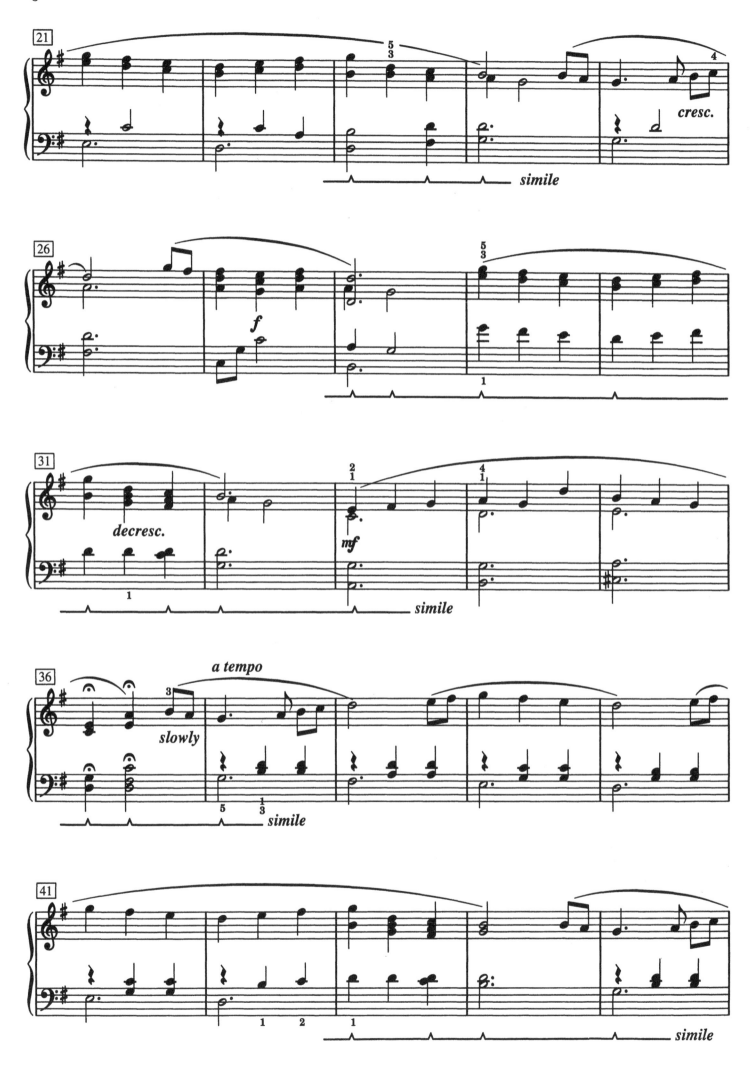

Angels We Have Heard On High

Traditional French Carol
Arranged by Jerry Ray

10

O Come, All Ye Faithful

Music by John Frances Wade
Arranged by Jerry Ray

*Taken from *For Unto Us a Child Is Born,*
from *The Messiah,* by G. F. Handel

Away in a Manger

James R. Murray
Arranged by Jerry Ray

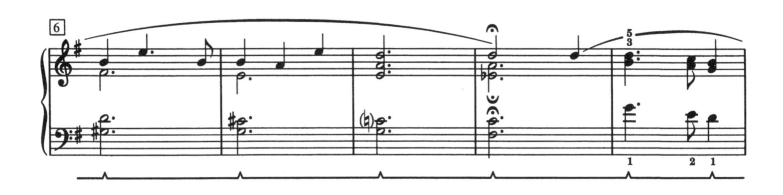

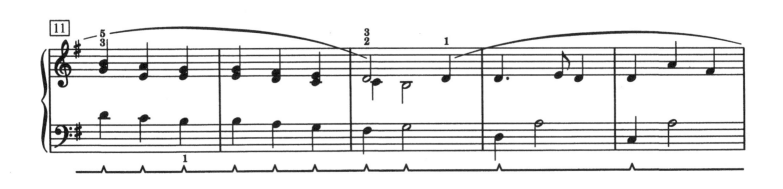

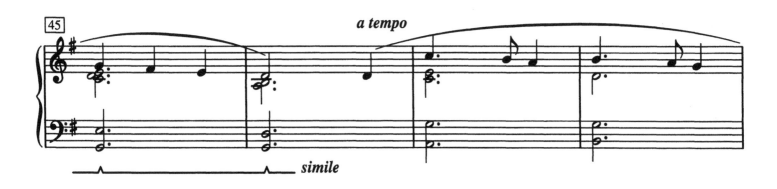

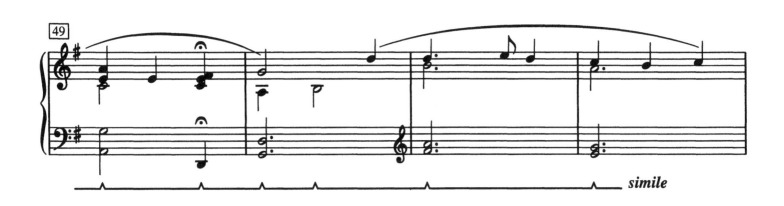

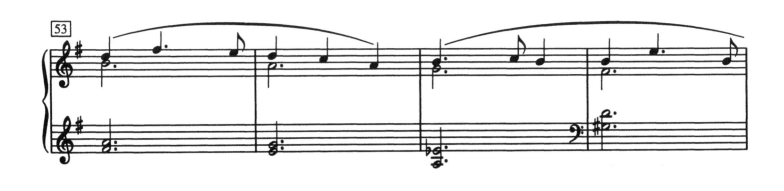

What Child Is This?

Old English Melody
Arranged by Jerry Ray

19

Deck the Halls

Traditional
Arranged by Jerry Ray

21

Jingle Bells

James Pierpont
Arranged by Jerry Ray

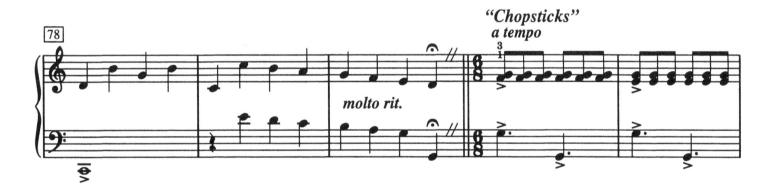

Joy to the World

G. F. Handel
Arranged by Jerry Ray

Majestically

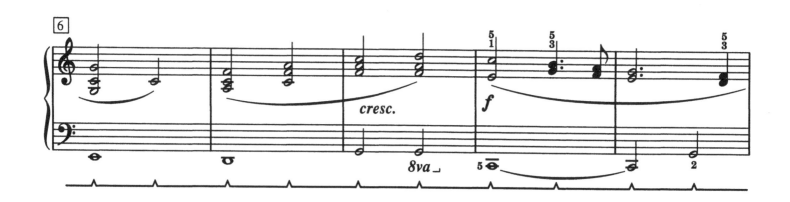

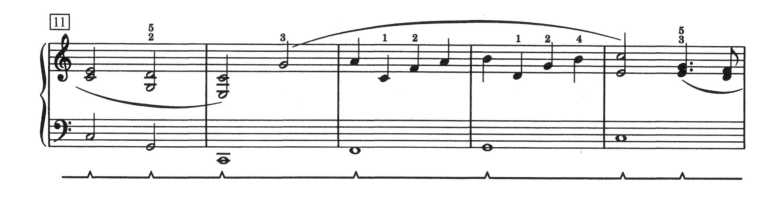

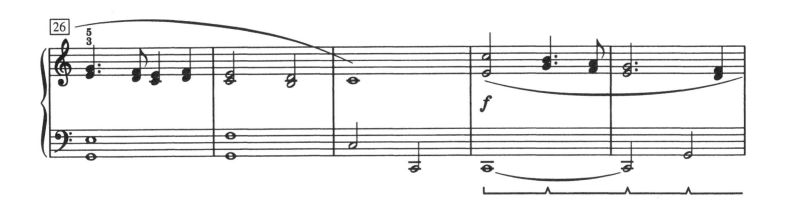

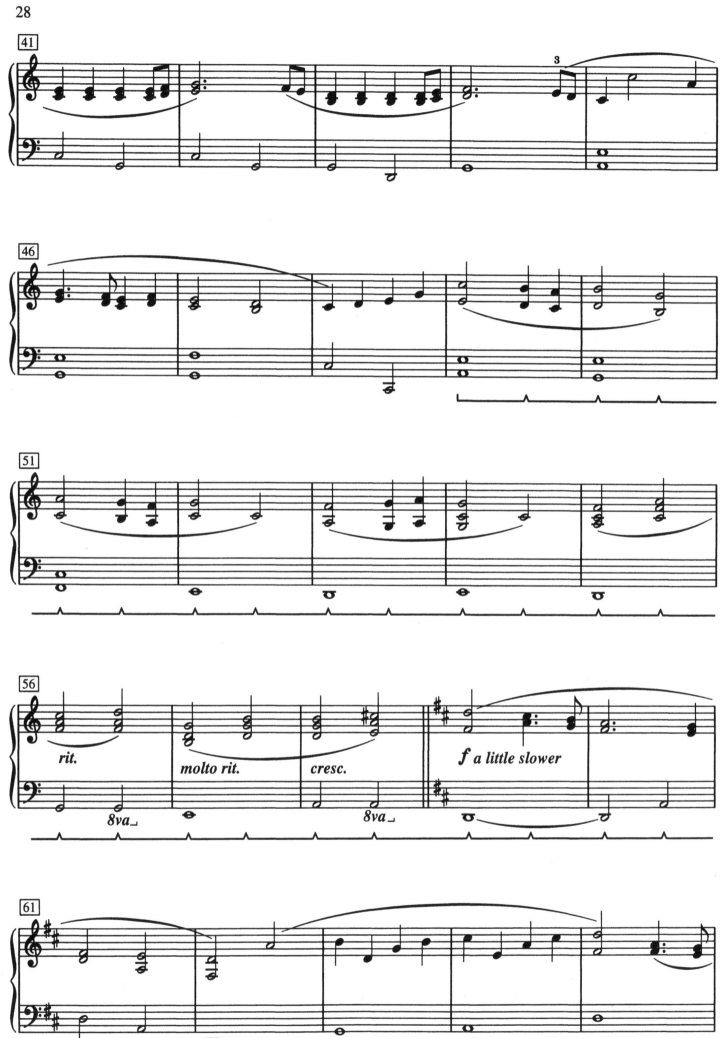

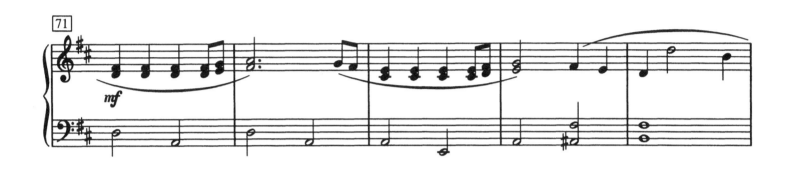

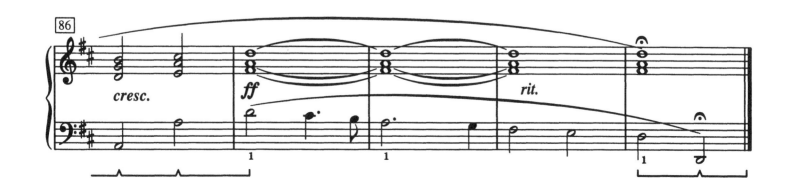

We Wish You a Merry Christmas

English Carol
Arranged by Jerry Ray

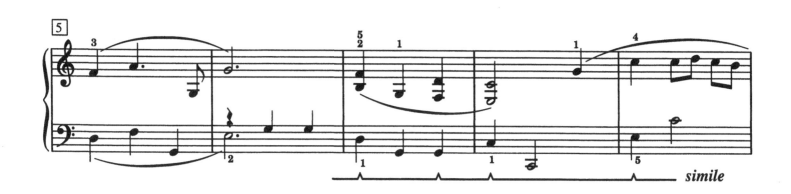

*Taken from *Emperor Waltz* by Johann Strauss

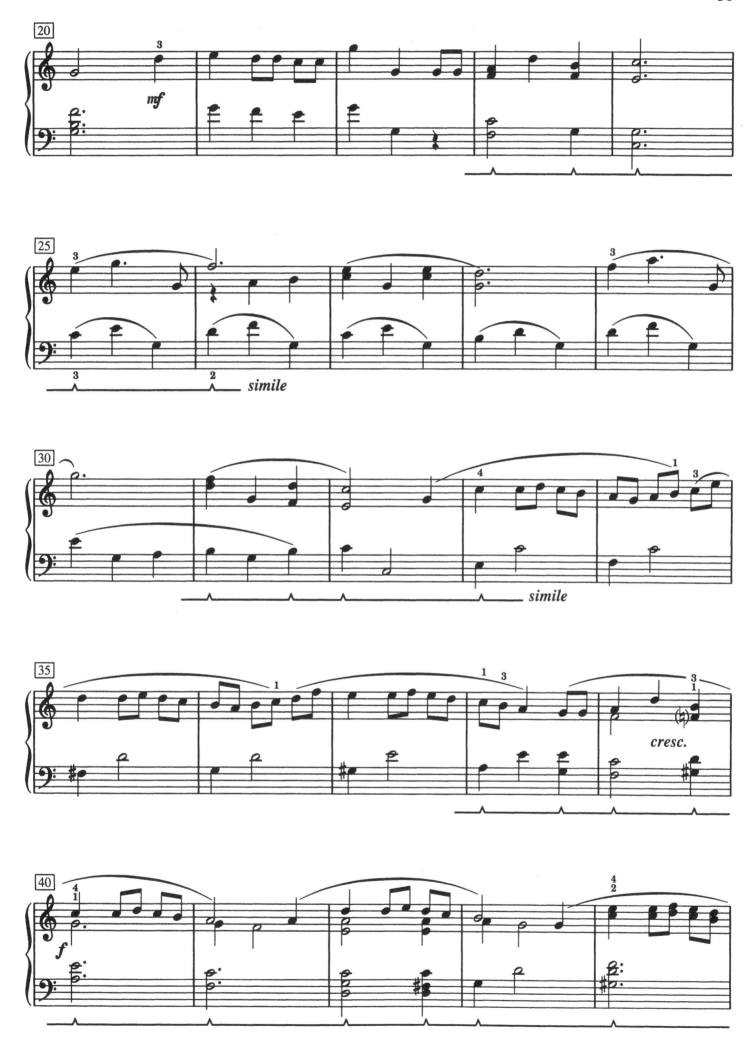

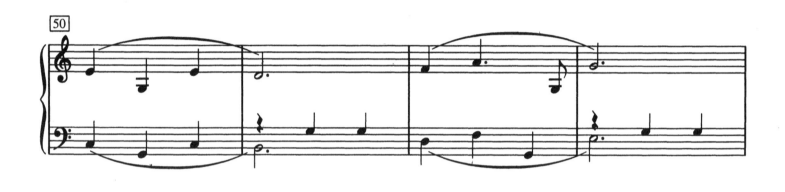